THE TRUSTWORTHY LEADER

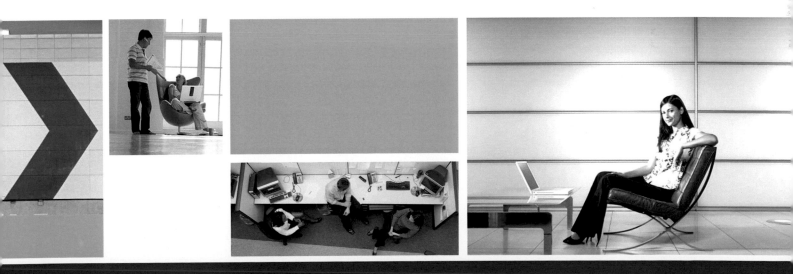

Pfeiffer

A Wiley Imprint

www.pfeiffer.com

Amy Lyman and Hal Adler

Self-Assessment: ISBN 978-0-470-90614-9

Acquiring Editor: Holly J. Allen

Director of Development: Kathleen Dolan Davies

Developmental Editor: Susan Rachmeler

Production Editor: Michael Kay

Editor: Rebecca Taff

Editorial Assistant: Michael Zelenko

Manufacturing Supervisor: Becky Morgan

Printed in the United States of America

PB Printing   10 9 8 7 6 5 4 3 2 1

This Self-Assessment will help you gauge how frequently you demonstrate the behaviors associated with trustworthy leadership.

Instructions: Review each statement below. Determine the frequency with which you demonstrate the behavior using the following scale, and write that number on the line provided:

1 = Never   **2** = Rarely   **3** = Sometimes   **4** = Often   **5** = Always

The results of this assessment will be most useful for you when you are straightforward and honest in your assessment. Don't over-analyze the items; enter your first response. Be sure to respond based on how you actually behave, not on how you *intend* to behave. When in doubt, think about how those around you might respond.

_____ 1.   I put meeting the needs of others ahead of personal self-interest.

_____ 2.   I take steps to bring diverse people and perspectives together.

_____ 3.   I am willing to take a step back and follow someone else's lead.

_____ 4.   I engage in open and honest communication.

_____ 5.   I identify a range of strengths and talents in others.

_____ 6.   I encourage dissenting points of view.

_____ 7.   I consistently treat others with care and respect.

_____ 8.   I acknowledge that every person's role in the organization is valuable.

_____ 9.   I explain how the work we do contributes to the success of others.

_____10.   I communicate with others at all levels of the organization.

_____11.   I know the career interests and aspirations of others.

_____12.   I support others in challenging decisions.

_____13.   I take the initiative to build open relationships with people at all levels of the organization.

_____14.   I seek out opportunities to interact with people with different backgrounds and points of view.

_____15.   I make an effort to get to know others as unique individuals.

1 = Never   2 = Rarely   3 = Sometimes   4 = Often   5 = Always

_____16.   I share information in ways that make it easy to understand and act upon.

_____17.   I explore possibilities and options to support the development of others.

_____18.   I help people access knowledge within the organization.

_____19.   I showcase the contributions of others more than what I have done.

_____20.   I encourage healthy conflict and vigorous debate.

_____21.   I help people across organizational levels and functions to work well together.

_____22.   I encourage employees to share information about challenges and solutions.

_____23.   I encourage people to try new things (even if they might be beyond their direct experience).

_____24.   I link goals and development to strategic initiatives.

_____25.   I encourage others to challenge me with questions about the organization's direction and strategy.

_____26.   I genuinely listen to new and different ideas.

_____27.   I support others in making decisions about their work.

_____28.   I am willing to consider and act on the good ideas of others.

_____29.   I ensure that every employee has a career path.

_____30.   I eliminate rules and practices that impede workflow.

_____31.   I use knowledge and skills to get things done, rather than power and authority.

_____32.   I strive to create a sense of belonging for everyone in the organization.

_____33.   I recognize collaborative efforts as well as results.

_____34.   I involve the most appropriate individuals in key decisions regardless of title or tenure.

_____35.   I spend time mentoring others.

_____36.   I allow those with the most knowledge about an issue to make decisions relative to it.

SCORING

Instructions:

1. Transfer your scores for each item to the appropriate column.

2. Total your scores in each column.

3. Add the six column scores together and divide by 6 to arrive at your Overall Trustworthy Leader score.

1_____	2_____	3_____	4_____	5_____	6_____
7_____	8_____	9_____	10_____	11_____	12_____
13_____	14_____	15_____	16_____	17_____	18_____
19_____	20_____	21_____	22_____	23_____	24_____
25_____	26_____	27_____	28_____	29_____	30_____
31_____	32_____	33_____	34_____	35_____	36_____
Total_____	Total_____	Total_____	Total_____	Total_____	Total_____
Honor	Inclusion	Valuing Followership	Sharing Information	Developing Others	Uncertainty & Opportunity
Overall Trustworthy Leader Score: Total all columns: _____ /6 =_____					

INTERPRETATION

Your scores provide some insight into the frequency with which you demonstrate the behaviors of trustworthy leaders.

Overall Score

Overall Trustworthy Leader scores of 25 to 30 indicate that you demonstrate the behaviors of trustworthy leaders with great consistency and likely experience success in terms of your interactions with others and business results.

Overall Trustworthy Leader scores of 19 to 24 indicate that you may make an effort to demonstrate the behaviors of trustworthy leaders frequently and might experience even greater results with an enhanced focus on individual assessment items you scored at 3 or lower.

Overall Trustworthy Leader scores of 18 or below indicate an opportunity for improvement. You do not demonstrate the behaviors of trustworthy leaders with sufficient consistency to get the most positive response **or** obtain the most benefits from your interactions with others. Focus on the one or two columns with your lowest scores immediately to begin building a trustworthy foundation.

Read the detailed sections that follow for more information about your scores and suggestions for optimizing your trustworthy leadership.

Honor

Area of Strength (25 to 30)

You see your leadership role as a privilege rather than an entitlement—a hallmark of trustworthy leaders. You are grateful for the opportunity to lead and fully acknowledge the responsibility that comes along with it. You recognize the importance of others and being of service to them. Seen as someone who demonstrates genuine caring, you work hard to develop give-and-take relationships with others regardless of their place on the organization chart. You appreciate that influence is more powerful than position and as a result cultivate commitment based on mutual respect and understanding. With honor as a strength, you may underestimate the value it brings—don't. Consciously cultivate this strength and even higher levels of trust will follow.

Solid Tendency upon Which to Build (19 to 24)

Although you see the responsibility for leading others as an honor, from time to time you may fall prey to the trappings associated with your leadership role. Challenge yourself to focus on learning more about what others need to be successful and meeting those needs rather than your own. This shift in perspective will return to you many-fold in terms of the trust it will build. Identify two or three leaders who exemplify honor to you. Schedule time to meet with them to explore their leadership philosophies and points of view and how those drive the choices they make on a day-to-day basis. Take what you learn from them and make it your own.

Opportunity for Improvement (18 and below)

Exhibiting honor is a building block for trustworthy leadership and as such is worthy of your immediate attention. Sometimes our sense of honor can be overshadowed by the pressure we feel to "get it right" and have all the answers. We try to show people that we are on top of everything. Yet a leader who is honored to be in the role needs to find ways to convey that to people. Start by considering your own perception of your role. Is leadership a right or a gift? Are you there to serve others or are they there to serve you? Honor comes from developing a core set of positive beliefs and perspectives about your role and those you lead and developing a deep appreciation about what you can accomplish with others as a leader. If you truly want to succeed as a trustworthy leader, then sharing your experience of how honored you are to be in your role is critical. Seek out a mentor or coach who will be willing to challenge and guide you to explore your awareness of leadership and the responsibilities that come with being a trustworthy leader.

Inclusion

Area of Strength (25 to 30)

Creating a strong sense of belonging for everyone in the organization you lead is a top priority—and, more than that, inclusion is very likely a bone-deep belief that drives much of what you do. You willingly challenge personal prejudices and the assumptions you may make about people and the role they play in achieving business results. You actively seek and are open to new ideas—no matter where they come from—and seek creative ways to share the benefits that come from success. Sharing your inclusive stance with others is an excellent way to be a role model and mentor for up-and-coming leaders. Continue to be a role model for broadly including others, and trust will build throughout the organization.

Solid Tendency upon Which to Build (19 to 24)

Although you acknowledge that everyone's role in the organization is valuable, you may not demonstrate that belief consistently on a day-to-day basis. Begin by reviewing the past week and analyze when your belief in inclusion was evidenced and what actions you took to promote inclusion. Then consider when it may have been in question, when assumptions or biases may have affected your interactions. Review the assessment items for inclusion and identify those that will help you close the gap between your intentions and what you actually do. Make a plan for when and how you will put those items into action. Ask for employee feedback. Inclusion, like beauty, is in the eye of the beholder.

Opportunity for Improvement (18 and below)

A philosophy of inclusion, along with exhibiting honor, is fundamental to building a strong foundation of trust with the people you lead. Given the role it plays in trustworthy leadership, a closer look at your inclusion philosophy is warranted. Challenge yourself to consider perceptions you hold about the value others bring to the organization, the roles they are able to play, and the contributions they are capable of making. Where do you look for new ideas? Who are your "go-to" people for creativity and innovation? What does that tell you about your own biases and assumptions? Are you aware of the limitations that come from interacting with a small group of people who are similar to you? Seek out people who have a reputation for inclusion and talk with them about how they perceive the value and contributions of those around them. Ask them about how they've become comfortable talking and interacting with people who are different from themselves. See where you can make even a small "attitude adjustment" and consciously put that into action. Chances are the results you realize will motivate additional reflection and action.

Valuing Followership

Area of Strength (25 to 30)

You are very clear that leaders are only as successful as the willingness of others to follow. Taking that a step further, you recognize that following is a choice people make . . . or don't. For you, leadership is not a solo act. Results come through people working with rather than for each other—accompanying each other to a shared destination. The personal relationships you build create connections that bond you with those you lead, demonstrating that you value the totality of their lives—not just the hours they put in at work. Although a strength, realize that valuing followership is a work in progress. Look to your followers for suggestions to enhance this capability.

Solid Tendency upon Which to Build (19 to 24)

You know you can't do it all on your own; however, in the throes of getting everything done you may not demonstrate this belief as consistently as you might. Review the assessment items for valuing followership and select the one that particularly resonates or sparks your interest. Commit to demonstrating that item once a day for the coming week. Set an alert or reminder for the same time each day to evaluate your effectiveness and the results you see. Putting a structure like this in place will make this element a stronger habit of mind over time.

Opportunity for Improvement (18 and below)

You may be making your life harder than it needs to be by believing you need to have all the answers. Trustworthy leaders understand that the most effective leadership is shared. Everyone has a time and place to step up and take on leadership responsibility based on his or her knowledge and expertise. You have to be willing to let others step up. Look out at your next week and the decisions and plans you anticipate making. Identify a specific situation for which you can offer someone a chance at leadership, to step back and follow his or her lead. Discuss the opportunity with that individual and collaborate on a plan to make it happen. It may take additional courage and self-discipline, but expanding this element of your Virtuous Circle will be well worth the effort.

Sharing Information

Area of Strength (25 to 30)

You understand that information sharing is as much about "how" you communicate as "what" you communicate. You appreciate that employees crave open, honest, actionable communication. And for you, information must go both ways. You frequently and consciously seek out the perspectives of others, in the process reinforcing your commitment to sharing information and building trust and business results. Continue to hone your skills, involving others in the development of information to share broadly, and model this critical leadership competency.

Solid Tendency upon Which to Build (19 to 24)

You make a sincere effort to engage in the meaningful exchange of information, ensuring that people can understand the information you are sharing and find ways to use it. You work toward open, honest communication that inspires action in others. You also put energy into engaging others by seeking out their ideas and input. Because this is an emerging tendency, a small amount of additional focus can deliver significant returns. Review the specific items in this column that you scored lower and identify just one action you could take each day to improve that score. You may be surprised at the results.

Opportunity for Improvement (18 and below)

Information sharing is an area that would benefit from additional reflection and focus. Working to understand the value of open, honest, and actionable communication at all levels of the organization may be a good first step. Team members and others will be better able to contribute to organizational success if they have the information they need to participate in the life of the organization. Review the specific items in this column and identify one strength (score of 4 or 5) that you could magnify even further with some additional attention. Also identify your lowest score in this column and discuss it with a colleague, coach, or your supervisor. Together brainstorm ways to demonstrate that behavior more frequently.

Developing Others

Area of Strength (25 to 30)

You are a developer of people and also support programs and practices that create a people-development culture in your team or organization. You commit the time and energy necessary to getting to know your employees, their strengths, and their talents. You encourage others to pursue their interests and goals. You appreciate the value of career paths . . . not just for high potentials but for every employee. Put your mentoring strength to use as you help others enhance their ability to develop others. By teaching them, you'll refine your own skills, build theirs, and enhance the quality of your trustworthy leadership.

Solid Tendency upon Which to Build (19 to 24)

You understand the importance of developing others and make a good effort toward making it happen by helping others to learn and grow each day. You try to get to know employees and understand who they are and what they want out of life. Make sure you apply these behaviors routinely to all employees. Identify the exceptional people developers in your organization and study what they do. Ask about their practices and strategies and make a commitment to try one or two of them. This will help you to develop others as well as provide you with ongoing development support for yourself.

Opportunity for Improvement (18 and below)

People development may not be getting the attention it deserves from you. Your support for developing others, whether by your own active involvement as a teacher and mentor or through your support of others' work, is an important way to ensure a sustainable pipeline of talent, meet organizational needs, and demonstrate trustworthy leadership. Review your lower scores for developing others and identify how to make improvements on those behaviors. Use those areas in which you received higher evaluations as strengths on which you can build, ensuring that you keep the focus on your positive skills in this area at the same time that you choose one area to make improvements. Start each day with a commitment to engage in at least one development-related conversation with an employee.

Uncertainty and Opportunity

Area of Strength (25 to 30)

You consistently demonstrate the behaviors that allow you and your team to leverage the uncertainties that are natural in organization life and harness the opportunities they bring. You ensure that people are free to disagree and challenge decisions. You cultivate and curate the knowledge required for success while minimizing the red tape that can impede exploration and creative results. You engage people in meaningful ways, always staying focused on the overall strategy. Review the individual assessment items within this column and identify one you want to give additional attention. Although it may already be a strength, consciously find ways to expand your use of the behavior—perhaps each day—and help your team take advantage of even more opportunities.

Solid Tendency upon Which to Build (19 to 24)

You probably appreciate that uncertainty and opportunity frequently go hand-in-hand. You make a fairly regular effort to create an environment in which people can challenge decisions, be involved when it makes sense, and access the knowledge and wisdom they need to succeed. But, given that uncertainty is a key factor in every leader's ability to be successful, you will benefit from additional attention to this leadership dimension. Review each assessment item from this column and identify the one that could have the greatest impact on your ability to work through uncertainty and realize critical organizational opportunities. Write that item on five adhesive notes and post them in key spots so you'll be reminded several times each day to consider and practice this one behavior.

Opportunity for Improvement (18 and below)

You may not be dedicating sufficient attention to the trustworthy leader behaviors that allow you to work with uncertainty and realize the opportunities that can be found in the choices you need to make as a leader. Given the volume of uncertainty that leaders are faced with in any organization today, developing the skills needed to move through uncertainty should be a priority. Make this concrete by identifying two real-life uncertainties that you and your team face. Then review each assessment item for this area and select the two behaviors that you believe could most powerfully help you to move through the uncertainty and discover opportunities. During a team meeting, share your ideas about the uncertainties facing the team and commit to the two behaviors that will be your new focus for guiding the team as you move forward. Ask team members to hold you accountable to your use of these two behaviors as part of your strategy for moving forward.